IMAGINE

Joseph Colombrita

Printed in the United States of America

First printing 2016

CreateSpace

4900 LaCross Road

North Charleston, SC 29406

USA

ISBN-13: 978-1532797064

ISBN-10: 1532797060

DEDICATION

this book is dedicated to everyone who

has followed their own imagination until

it became a reality. a special thanks to my

mother kathleen and my father phil. also

to my brother chris and sister lori. and

my niece mikayla and daughter isabella.

to everyone who has supported my work

thank you so much. without you i am nothing.

For Isabella Marie

imagine

IMAGINE

a collection of poems

"it has never been about the money.

it has always been about the passion

to write and tap into my emotions.

this is my gift and my words will

be unwrapped one poem at a time"

-Joseph Colombrita

in memory to all the people we lost way too soon from carteret . this is for you and your names will live on forever.

beautiful soul

she was beautiful
but her looks
never stood a
chance compared
to how
breathtaking
her soul was

blinders

it's like i
have blinders
on to the
rest of the
world
and all i
see is you
your soul speaks
to mine
you should never
have to
wonder
you should know
by
now

ghost

your love was

a ghost that

you wanted me

to believe in

without ever

seeing it

your reflection

not loving what

you see when your

staring at your

own reflection

will be the

greatest love

you ever

lose

smile

**don't depend on
the world to make
you smile but smile
like the world
depends
on it**

<u>holy grail</u>

her beauty was

a work of art

but her soul

was the holy

grail

angel of hope

i can hear her speaking
to me as i internally
take in her every word
my smile awakens to the
echoes of her voice
her thoughtful nature
restores my faith
my intuition tells me
to follow her vibe to
that place we both
long to be
a palace of love and hope
i need to feel her presence
just as much as she needs mine
we are a perfect symphony of
music for the inspired and
the hopeless
i wait for her to bleed her heart
alongside of mine as our emotions
melt into the sea together
she is special
my angel of hope

mine just a sky

i saw the stars

in your eyes

and mine

just a sky

that needed

them

wounded heart

my heart was wounded
a fresh scar of heartbreak
but it was your love
and compassion that
nurtured my soul
back to health
sewing my wound
closed just so i
could love another
lifetime

graveyard of souls

i have a graveyard

full of souls i loved

even though they are

dead to me i swear

their ghosts knock

on my souls door

and runaway every

once in a while

just for the fun

of it or maybe to

remind me that any

kind of love you ever

had never dies

an ocean

my mind has become
an ocean and the
thoughts of you
come in waves
but knowing your
not mine i am
slowly drowning
with each wave
that crashes

imperfect composition

a mental expedition
an every night tradition
wondering what's missing
thoughts free of admission
my mind is in the right position
silently i begin to listen
it's my act of contrition
only with gods permission
so this is my own rendition
until it adds up like addition
following my own ambitions
with a constant repetition
a poet and musician
with curious suspicions
this is just my definition
of a imperfect composition

broken like me

and i will never understand

how someone as beautiful as

you loves someone so

broken like me

frozen

when she kissed me
for the first time
i froze
because i didn't
know if i would
ever feel this
good ever again

loving again

it's never easy
to love again
but when it
finally stands
in front of you
make sure their
heart stands
behind it with
the same intention

lonely highway

my mind is crowded

with bumper to bumper

traffic of my thoughts

but it is a lonely highway

that i drive on

scars

i use my words

to cover up the

scars and use

my scars to

create the words

destiny awaits

an empty room
pen full of ink
my house of god
quiet time to think
deep breaths
very few movements
always more room
for my self improvement
that light that shines
i find it hard to see
until you let it go
what is will always be
i am love
i love you dearly
our lips touching
i envision this clearly
here i will be waiting
even if it exists merely
the night is getting late
for my destiny awaits

perfect harmony

our souls
became
the
perfect
harmony
of love
in a
world
so out
of tune

so in love

we were so in love

that when we looked

up at the sky together

the stars we used to

wish upon gazed at us

and envied what true

love felt like

broken pieces

most who come into
your life will sweep
the broken pieces
under the rug
and a real friend
will notice something
wrong with the rug
and pick up those
broken pieces
without asking

dancing soul

my soul dances

to your hypnotic

rhythm and i dance

to it like the

world isn't watching

partner in crime

i'm a lover and
not a fighter
because you
should
never have to
fight to
keep
someones
love
just have to
love to
keep it

just in time

love doesn't come

on your time

but just in time

<u>types</u>

i have been
around
you for a
few years
and never
thought
you were
"my type"
but you have
become
"the type"
i have fallen
for and
i've become
"the type"
too shy to
tell you

mother nature

and when someone
buries themselves
up to their neck in lies
the tide of mother
nature will not be
so forgiving

tip toe

every night i
tip toe
around my
loneliness
and i try
not to
wake him

keep being you

and if nothing good
came out of today
it's ok
when tomorrow
comes you will do
what you have
always done
keep fighting
and believing
but most
importantly
keep
being
you

gypsy soul

she was a young bohemian
with an old soul
a timeless treasure filled
with fire and the essence of
mother earth
her head was in the clouds
but her feet planted on
the ground
her eyes glimmered of
emeralds and they sparkled
with mystery
her secrets hidden away
behind a mysterious smile
i am digging her vibes and
want to roam the world
alongside of her spirit
my soul is whispering
to yours and if you
listen closely you can
hear the rhythms of
the spanish guitar
as our spirits dance
with the moon and
the stars
until she peeks her face
from behind the curtain
again i will dreaming of
you my gypsy soul

stepping stone

i just wanted to
be your rock
but all I ever was
to you was your
stepping stone

art gallery

each piece of you at
one time was just
a rough draft that
became a sketch of
hope or a portrait of
pain hanging alongside
of a sculpture of your dreams
and most will just pass you
by but some will stop and look
briefly at those beautiful
emotions you have painted
and one day some one will
walk through your gallery
and fall in love with every
piece of art that you are

heart on my sleeve

i still wear my heart
on my sleeve with
all it's scars exposed
to let others know
i'm too strong to
change who i am

dreams

it makes no
difference what
dream you have
and the world
will doubt you
but believing in
your own dream
makes a world
of difference

kindness

you were blind
to my
kindness
but my
kindness
never looses
it's
sight on the
reasons why
i am

soul queen

she had the beauty
of a queen but it
was her soul
that wore
the crown

open your heart

opening your heart
to the world
doesn't mean
you have to
let the world
sew it closed
for you

if her thoughts

she has been through so much
only if her thoughts could speak
hiding behind a wall of doubt
yet on her face a smile she keeps
bad memories are buried so deep
hoping someday she'll outgrow it
these scars she keeps hidden
so others she meets never knows it
it's the only way she knows to cope
doing it for her own protection
that mirror that once was her altar
she no longer can look at her reflection
keeping all her thoughts a hostage
so scared to ever let them go free
her self esteem is so far gone
the light in the tunnel she can't see
most will never know what she's been through
yet they will gossip and critique
inside her screams are deafening
only if her thoughts could speak

come and go

take your time
play it slow
the day will come
and the day will go
just like the rain
so does the pain
it just seems to know
the day will come
and the day will go
all of the sorrow
will have to wait
till tomorrow
it is meant to be so
the day will come
and the day will go

her smile

she had a smile

that could light

up the room but

had a soul that

could light up

the world

in my arms

i never wanted

you to fall for me

until you were

ready to land

in my arms

so much more

she was a lot
stronger than
she believed
and so much
more beautiful
than he ever
made her believe

promise the world

if they promise you
the world just make
sure the world they
promise you doesn't
just revolve
around them

maybe if you

maybe if you stared
into her eyes with
love and compassion
with the same intensity
that your eyes always
undressed her with
she would still be here
to gaze into your
eyes forever

"someday"

it may just be

another day to

some but it will

be that"someday"

they always

dreamed about

for others

enemies

your enemies smile
will be just as charming
as your friends but
looking into their eyes
you will know
the difference

deepest depths

someone who really
loves you will swim
by your side
through the
deepest depths
and
not try to
drown you in it

break the chains

you've become your own prisoner
trapped inside of the walls you built
holding it all inside is how you hide
torturing yourself with all of the guilt
the love you once had has drifted away
silent screams that no one hears
wearing the mask of a happy person
so they can't see your endless tears
you've been trapped in the darkness
that you don't believe there is light
swimming in the depths of loneliness
feeling like the only star in the night
you must remember that your never alone
the sun shines after all of the rain
so love yourself the way you deserve
or you will never be able to break the chains

listen to them

don't just look

into her eyes

listen to them

burning desire

she is my burning
desire in my soul
and with each thought
of her the flames
grew more intense

my kindness

they said my
kindness was
a weakness
till i
killed them
with it

i might be

don't compare me
to a past love that
didn't last forever
i might be that
forever

<u>positive picture</u>

don't expect a
positive picture
when your
in the dark
developing
the negatives

pass my time

i used to think
in time my
thoughts of
you would
pass but all
they do is
pass all my
time

gone forever

if she looses interest
in you there is a chance
she may come back
but if she looses
respect for you
she will be gone forever

the boss

when my mind tells
me to give up on
loving you
my heart steps in
to remind me who
the boss is

in the end

in the end
i knew no
matter how
hard i tried
to hold on
that fate had
already let
us go

stars in the sky

we are all
stars in
the sky
and i
envied the
one closest
to you

recaptured

the style of the unique
waiting for the pen to speak
behind the curtain we peek
looking for the answers we seek
my boutique put on full display
some of it might be cliché
maybe a lesson for the stray
to keep it you must give it away
i get visions of many dreams
endless thoughts amongst the streams
once the sun reveals it's beams
hope becomes a familiar theme
redeeming heaven from hell
darkness becomes a shade of pastel
round and round on the carousel
in a trance deep under a spell
a farewell to the past tense
the feeling becomes so intense
as it all starts to make sense
a pretense of a new chapter
letting go of the internal rapture
even when your spirit is fractured
with love it can always be recaptured

just a reminder

the stars i used

to wish upon

for your love

have become

just a reminder

of how out of

reach your love was

the reason

you became the reason
that people ask me
why am i smiling so
much and a few
of them
wished someone
smiled about them
the way i do for you

your song

you played the
strings so
beautiful that
i danced to the
lies and when
you looked up
just as your song
was ending the
dance floor
was empty

life sentence

even though you
were the one
guilty of cheating
it is my heart that
is doing
a life sentence

they only see

they only see her pretty face
and get lost in her eyes
but it is all an illusion
they never see the tears she cries
she knows when to smile
so no one will ever know
just to hide all the hurt
she never learned to let go
but she never gives up
through all of life's stress
and she keeps her head high
because she knows she's doing her best

one hit wonder

you were a medley

of love songs to me

and i was your

one hit wonder

spirit dancer

she's my spirit dancer
a gypsy soul with lips
full of passion
and the depths of her
eyes would make the
oceans jealous
she wanders through my
thoughts but will stay
a lifetime

never too old

your never too old

to dream

and dreaming

never gets old

universal souls

i love the way her hair
covers her emerald
eyes in disguise
and i want to lick the
sin from her lips
pulling her closer with
my hands on her hips
feeling her heartbeat just
as fast as mine
slowly kissing her neck as
she moves her hair and
her eyes start to roll in
pleasure
just letting go in the moment
as our skin burns with passion
and the teasing and pleasing
leads me needing to feel
her deep and her wanting me
deep inside her just pleasuring
our minds just as much as our
bodies
and as we exhaled our ecstasy
our souls connected with
the universe that night

<u>flawless</u>

she was full of
flaws but you
would never
know with a smile
that was flawless

can't buy love

he wanted to

buy your love

by spending

money and

all you wanted

was someone to

spend time

small gifts

sometimes it's
the small gifts
in life that have
the biggest
presence

so removed

some days i
feel so removed
from life but
knowing you are
here for me puts
back the life in me

<u>secret whispers</u>

it is no coincidence

we both have been

thinking of each other

it's our souls

whispering to

one another

late night show

it's our late night ritual
same place same time
taking you on a journey
through different states of mind
me not knowing what to write
then my words begin to sing
our energies start to connect
 just as i begin to spread my wings
going to that place we all love
flying under the electric sky
we are constellations aligned
in our own galaxy just you and i
it allows us to just relax for now
amongst our dreams we are chasing
a chance to escape for a while
our inner thoughts slowly embracing
each night that we spend together
our hearts start to dance nice and slow
the more we get to know each other
the greater our connection grows
your always invited to ride along
or take a seat in the front row
thanks for taking the time again
and coming out to our late night show

a stranger

love became
a stranger
and the
only thing
that became
familiar
was the
loneliness

could never be

i just want to love
you like he never
did and you to
love me like you
never did and
you and i to be
that forever they
could never be
for us

<u>numbers don't lie</u>

you told me you
loved me a hundred times
and was never in
love with me once
the numbers don't lie
only you do

pale moonlight

in a deep meditation
quietly i just sit
the ceremony has begun
now that the fire is lit
morning is back to sleep
and that's when the owl awakes
transcending my vibrations
with each thought that i make
soft music begins to play
just to set the mood right
so come dance with me
under the pale moonlight
my inner spirits are speaking
it is not a game of chance
levitating my body
to a deep hypnotic trance
embracing the warm feeling
as it takes hold of my soul
a deep breathe than I exhale
as it begins to take control
i am right here beside you
no need to ever be afraid
we are the spirit dancers
our destiny is already laid
the evening is all ours
so in love with the night
until we rendezvous again
under the pale moonlight

way she hid

i was attracted

to her smile

not because

how happy

she looked

but how well

she hid

her pain

fools gold

your heart of
gold was made
of fools
and it tarnished
mine into a fool
like yours

just as sick

i think lonely

is just as sick

of me as

i am lonely

used to care

i used to care
how the world
viewed me until
i realized
how i viewed
the world was
more important

world around me

i built a wall so
big that i can
no longer see
the world
around
me

when the ink dries

visions of words
i try to vividly capture
hours of endless writings
till my mind becomes enraptured
a ripple effect of my conscious
i am constantly chasing
each thought connects
becoming a sudden revelation
still i am searching
to find the perfect words
my inner thoughts are so loud
yet i'm so shy and reserved
emotions start pouring out
without any resistance
a mirror of my reflection
shadows of my existence
finding my purpose
some meaning of relevance
composing a masterpiece
of divine eloquence
observing intensely
just a brief engagement
a moment of time
so fresh and fragrant
it becomes so intimate
my depths run so deep
memories i kept cherished
are mine to forever keep
when the ink finally dries
from this same pen
another chapter begins
soon as this one ends

dominoes

we are all

just dominoes

lined up for

love and keep

getting

knocked

down

soliloquy serenade

am i saying too much
or too little to understand
don't want my words to wash away
like a castle that is made out of sand
if only you could hear me
without uttering a single world
silent thoughts that i whisper
hoping that they never go unheard
i wander in my mind constantly
with a heart filled with love
i am dancing with the angels
gazing at the stars up above
so before the night ends
and the music begins to fade
i will hold onto this feeling
until the last note is played
for if tomorrow never comes
the right choice i have made
sharing my thoughts that i hide
singing to you my soliloquy serenade

my master

**loneliness became
my master and
i became it's
biggest servant**

not enough time

there is not

enough time

in the day

for all the

thoughts of

you i have

love

love never quits

love always tries

love is forever

love it never dies

a lil crush

wonder if I surprised you
but I am not in a rush
i just wanted you to know
that on you i have a little crush
i am a hopeless romantic
and maybe a little naive
thinking you would feel the same
yet i still want to believe
hope you will get to read this
and maybe it will make you blush
but I had to let you know
for a while i've had a lil crush

for love to be

and maybe we just

need for love to

be what it is

not what we

always want

it to be

tunnel vision

baby it's like
i have tunnel
vision and the
rest of the world
doesn't exist
only you and i

someday

someday it will be
nice to come home
to someone instead
of an empty bed
and another poem
about what lonely
feels like

kapha

ancient past time
weeping and wailing
crystal ship is sailing
life's storms are hailing
steps are taken
spirits have awaken
god given ability
deep thoughts of tranquility
information consumption
avoiding self destruction
function amongst the highest
in the shadows of my shyness
expressing a feeling
internal healing
at times too revealing
the pain we are concealing
appealing for some
kneeling towards the sun
a feeling to run
dealing with what comes
vibrant sensations
beautiful interpretations
from a lost paradise
selfless choice of sacrifice
creatures of habit
anxiety running rapid
if the jacket fits
then wear it
this is too important
for me not to share it

in the end

in the end
i knew no
matter how
hard i tried
to hold on
that fate had
already let
us go

miles between us

the miles
between us
could never
compete with
how far my
heart is
willing to go

thought of you

sometimes just a
thought of you
or seeing your
picture makes
the loneliness
disappear if
only for a
few moments

keep being you

the funny thing about living
is that nothing will be given
it all starts with the power of mind
what you seek you shall find
just a little hope is all you need
putting trust in your faith to succeed
all of those who held you back to achieve
are the same ones who will all soon believe
do not follow in the trails of a heathen
only darkness it will lead you through
keep on walking towards the light
until that light finally shines on you
whatever comes your way make do
no matter what others say keep being you

all alone

and when she finally
left me all alone
i realized i was
all alone the
whole time

cruel lies

you always had
a kind way of
telling cruel
lies and in your
case kindness was
your biggest
weakness

never too old

your never too

old to change

only too stubborn

endless thoughts

my words

may be few

but my thoughts

of you are endless

just to see mine

on those days
she didn't feel
like smiling she
did anyway just
so she could
see mine

your lips

when i kissed
your lips for the
first time i felt so
free but i wanted
to be locked up
with them forever

but mine

i was able
to call
her every
beautiful
word to
describe
her from
afar
but
one
mine

perfect for you

all of my own words and nothing is quoted
had this in my head so i sat down and wrote it
i speak in my silence hoping you can hear me
just my thoughts alone with no conspiracy theory
question everything or except all the answers
i am amused and soak in all the witty banter
how you will perceive this that all depends
is this just the beginning or the beginning of the end
sending my hope to you free of charge
so dream small until they become large
live it and breathe it for this is who you are
it is never out of reach or never too far
i know what it feels like when life gets hard
sweating the small stuff you must disregard
never rush in and let nature take it's time
out from the darkness and making it shine
erasing my mind so i don't hear a sound
it is my sanctuary and becomes so profound
for a moment time and space stand still
basking in my silence of my own free will
it may not be so perfect
but if you keep a perfect view
then the perfection you see
will always be perfect enough for you

<u>your forever</u>

i just want to be
your forever that
they all promised
they would be

without you

just remember i
didn't become
everything i am
today with you
but without
you

loved the same

i'm never too tired

to love but i'm

exhausted of wanting

to be loved the same

her beautiful soul

those dreams you dream of
special moments you forever hold
probably never hear it like you should
but i know you have a beautiful soul
always putting others before you
wearing your heart on your sleeve
you give hope to the hopeless
just who you are makes others believe
your positive light shines so bright
i know this world can be so cruel
the patience and care you display
always smiling and keeping your cool
so willingly to give everything you have
expecting nothing to come in return
loving like no one is watching
acting as if you have never been burned
i can feel your whole aura just glow
it is something that is to be admired
the way you just keep pushing on
with all of your passion,drive and desire
so keep being you my love
that style you have never gets old
your beauty that's on your outside
is just a reflection of your beautiful soul

<u>temptation</u>

she was beautiful
surrounded by
temptation but
it wasn't her
beauty that
i fell for but
the way she
handled the
temptation

dream come true

visualize the dream
believe in the dream
you are the dream
and when you least
expect it you will
become someones
dream come true

<u>illusions</u>

**maybe your love
for me was all an
illusion but your
kisses were magic**

internal dialogue

this is my natural gift
from the warm morning sun
silence within myself
is what needs to be done
engaged in internal dialogue
as my consciousness grows
i know i am here right now
tomorrow nobody ever knows
a thirst for more knowledge
always some room to drink more
so i start sipping slowly
from mother natures reservoir
outside of my self
looking at my own reflection
loving who i see
embracing my own affection
a connection i have made
thoughts i hold in my memory
i am at peace with myself
soaking in all of life's energy
remember me only for a moment
then let my spirit pass through
don't be so judgmental
is all i will ask of you
only half of what i could be
until the day i am whole
blessings to us all
have mercy on our souls

just a number

i was always just

a number to you

but never the one

never fade away

and i know
someday our
looks will fade
away but the
beauty of our
love never
has to

her heart

i chased after
her body to hell
not realizing it
was her heart
that would
lead me
to heaven

whiskey sipping

walking down west 57th st
brown bagging it
i am tired
still buzzing though
whiskey sipping
sirens blaring
ah feels like home
loose change ringing
swaying through city blocks
the night time
is my lifeline
hey can you spare some change
bottle half empty
my outlook half full
good times
new rhymes
i ain't tripping
just whiskey sipping

<u>one day at a time</u>

take it easy stop moving so fast
hard times will come and they will pass
don't let it get you down
your time is coming back around
everything will play out fine
as long as you take it one day at a time

so does the tears

when you fall

out of love

so does the

tears

to the moon

the crater you left
in my heart is proof
i was willing to go
to the moon and back
for your love

after you

after

    you

       there

          never

            was

the first one

you were the first one

who truly made my

heart smile to match

the one on my face

the right way

the thoughts of
my broken heart
are a painful
reminder that
i loved you
the right way

what her eyes hide

she flaunted
her smile just
to divert your
attention from
what her eyes
fought to hide

posing

you were an atheist
posing as a saint
and tried making
me believe that
i didn't exist
either

drifts back

her loved drifted
away and yet
i still sit here
staring at the
waves hoping
her love drifts
back to my heart

promises

why promise them
the world when
the world promises
you nothing

deep wounds

the wounds
are deep
and my smile
distracts you
from looking

a gift

she said i
am deep and
have a gift
with my words
but secretly i
admired her gift
of being happy

hold me

don't tell me

everything is

going to be

alright just

hold me until

i am

gypsy sonata

it is my time
the dark night draws me in
silence starts to fade
soon as the spanish rhythm begins
dancing in my head
spirits of a lost armada
an outer body experience
this is my gypsy sonata
i am all alone
as my conscious elevates
to my highest of peaks
internally i begin to celebrate
my body is swaying
the sounds are so soothing
a devilish grin
finding this all so amusing
feeling so alive
in a trance from the vibe
i am the gypsy
from a nomadic tribe
my mind is roaming
guided by the spirits protection
the shadow of the night
begins to cast my reflection
it lets me love
one with time and space
once the moments gone
time can no longer replace
a selfish journey
a fire burns eternally
this path i am traveling
searching for my own eternity
i must carry on
carousing with the pixies
a moonlight sonata
for i am the gypsy

stayed forever

it was the ones

who told her

they love her

that came and went

but the one who

showed her

stayed forever

feels right

don't just do
it because you
thought it was
right but do it
because it
feels right

easy and free

they think these
words come so
easy and free
but the scars
that these words
were born from
are constant
reminders that
nothing comes
easy or free

never will be

you will
always
be my
one and
only and i
will only
ever be
the one
that never
will be

someone like you

it wasn't that
you deserved
better but
they never
deserved
someone
like
you

here and now

surrounded in silence for the mind to meditate
opening up my soul for my thoughts to levitate
they leave my body but the body never leaves
best believe there is no honor amongst thieves
it's all about perception and what you perceive
when death comes knocking then everyone believes
the karma you receive from all those you deceived
will comeback someday quietly like christmas eve
i'm leaving on the next plane or the next freight train
going nowhere strapped to this ball and chain
 i only blame myself for this is my own trip
only i can speak for myself from my own lips
no quick fix no quick high nothing to stick by
feel the rain coming fast under this thick sky
forecast still cloudy with no sight of sunlight
like i'm caught in between a good and evil gunfight
dodging bullets of death with every last breathe
just me myself and i is all i really have left
see ya on the rebound if i ever make it back
my final act will be a illusion to fade to black
bags are packed till I reach my final destination
i have a fifty fifty chance according to my estimations
my patience are my rock so i wait patiently
go out on my own terms and bow out gracefully
you must be mistaken me for some other person
that's on you and will have to carry that burden
waiting till the final curtain to take my final bow
the curtain is falling so i will make it here and now

perfectly poetic

writing the perfect
poem about you
will never compare
to how perfectly
poetic your soul is

always chasing

your always chasing

the one who doesn't

love you and never

wait to be caught

by the one who does

professional heart breaker

i never had a chance
i was an amateur in love
getting hustled by a
professional heart breaker

real men

whoever says

real men don't

cry never had

a love like yours

magic tricks

your love was
just an illusion
and i always
been a sucker
for magic tricks

you thought

you thought
by telling me
i love you
over and over
that it would
distract me
from leaving
but it only
reminded me
of how much
you never
showed me

be like you

not everyone is
willing to give
like you
love like you
sacrifice and
forgive like you
and not everyone
will like you but
you always
inspire
others to be
like you

lullaby

sing me a lullaby
as the sweet sounds cascades
it sounds so beautiful
until the silence begins to fade

sing me a lullaby
a melody that's so serene
enchanted by the rhythm
taking me into a dream

sing me a lullaby
as the night begins to fall
gently whisper in my ear
until i'm at peace and enthralled

sing me a lullaby
if tomorrow never comes true
sing for me one last time
as i bid you sweet adieu

if only you

if only you
could commit
to love again
the same way
you have accepted
to being lonely

the peace

once i stopped
looking for
the missing
piece is when
i found the
peace

<u>being strong</u>

i used to
think by
holding
on i was
being
strong
and when
i let go i
realized
what being
strong really
is

letter to heaven

i'm writing this letter in hopes you hear me
not a day goes by that i don't feel you near me
i guess it's true that nothing gold can last
it's been some time now since you passed
i long to hear your voice or see your face
trying to convince myself your in a better place
my heart is still broken and it's too deep to grasp
i try to smile but i'm just hiding behind a mask
yet i am so grateful for all the things you did
i often flashback to when i was a little kid
when the world was so new with no pain
since you have been gone nothing is the same
so many emotions just run through my mind
wishing that we could have spent a lot more time
i know they say everything happens for a reason
nights i spent crying i have a hard time believing
but i'm trying to be strong just like you always were
then i just breakdown and everything becomes a blur
you taught me to be honest so i can't lie
when your spirit passed a piece of me died
i used to confide in you about all of my dreams
you always encouraged me that i could achieve
to believe in myself and listen to my heart
never turned your back on me when i fell apart
teaching me to be courteous respectful and kind
you gave me visions of hope when i was blind
no words that i write could ever truly express
as the tears drip on these pages as i try to confess
just to have you in my life I know i was blessed
it's a way for me to heal and get it off my chest
my broken heart is still mending from all we been through
i hope someday you get my letter to heaven just for you

<u>footprints</u>

walk the road
of happiness
and the
footprints
you leave
behind
others
will find
hope in

inspirations and thanks: bob marley, frank sinatra, jim morrison, the doors, irvington, n.j, carteret, n.j, breakin, nas, illmatic, mobb deep,imagine,langston hughes,boredom cult, biggdoggstrongg, rocco, estas tonnes, rutgers football, isabella marie, ex girlfriends, amy winehouse, back to black, howard stern, eloisa, connie, sharon, meaghan, dr desai, dr shah, dr faruggia,liza, chrisitne b, mindy, dj duke,grizzly rip, rm drake, dru anthony, those who always support my work michele n,christine b,nicole l,laurie p,jennifer n,maggie w,tatuchick,ahd5814,journeybleu,haleymacleod,haciendatx ,k.h.r,thieverycorporation, esq,werenotthatdiffrent,mattbwriting,ajwilliam,bmymuse, rationalmadness,lovinm,glenorozco,notmikmiswear,mom mbywords,moenyc718,dkmclainpoetess,babyguppy,kellyro ssi,mmopoetry,letmejustsay,writerliz,jmcoffee.harmony2g race,mbvictoria,eddiesatelier,ittmcmahon,nmshami,words byrose,sensual,claudette,jessica musings,piecesoflonging,poetictemptation,przfiona,jennife r t,mackill,suzettespics,placidsensualist,lonelyisthe heart,missmieshka,vanessalocampo,greybirmingham,make blackoutpoetry,frankie ewize,stevie wonder,jimmy roselli,and everyone else i forgot to mention love you mom,dad,chris,lori,mikayla,isabella....................

Made in the USA
Middletown, DE
29 May 2016